Is This Really My Family?

Relating to Your Relatives

ABDO
Publishing Company

Strong, Beautiful Girls

Is This Really My Family?

Relating to Your Relatives

by Ashley Rae Harris

Content Consultant
Vicki F. Panaccione, PhD
Licensed Child Psychologist
Founder, Better Parenting Institute

Credits

Published by ABDO Publishing Company, 8000 West 78th Street, Edina, Minnesota 55439. Copyright © 2009 by Abdo Consulting Group, Inc. International copyrights reserved in all countries. No part of this book may be reproduced in any form without written permission from the publisher. The Essential Library™ is a trademark and logo of ABDO Publishing Company.

Printed in the United States.

Special thanks to Dr. Vicki Panaccione for her expertise and guidance in shaping this series.

Editor: Amy Van Zee
Copy Editor: Patricia Stockland
Interior Design and Production: Nicole Brecke
Cover Design: Becky Daum

Library of Congress Cataloging-in-Publication Data
Harris, Ashley Rae.
  Is this really my family? : relating to your relatives / by Ashley Rae Harris.
      p. cm. — (Essential health : strong, beautiful girls)
  Includes index.
  ISBN 978-1-60453-101-5
  1. Teenage girls—Family relationships. 2. Teenage girls—Psychology. 3. Parent and teenager. 4. Family. 5. Interpersonal relations. I. Title.

  HQ798.H359 2008
  646.7'808352—dc22

                                        2008012105

Contents

Meet Dr. Vicki

Throughout the series Strong, Beautiful Girls, you'll hear the reassuring, knowledgeable voice of Dr. Vicki Panaccione, a licensed psychologist with more than 25 years of experience working with teens, children, and families. Dr. Vicki offers her expert advice to girls who find themselves in the difficult situations described in each chapter.

Better known as the Parenting Professor™, Dr. Vicki is founder of the Better Parenting Institute™ and author of *Discover Your Child* and *What Your Kids Would Tell You . . . If Only You'd Ask!* You might have seen her name quoted in publications such as the *New York Times*, *Family Circle*, and *Parents* magazine.

While her credentials run deep, perhaps what qualifies her most to advise girls on everything from body image to friendship to schoolwork is that she's been there, so she can relate. "I started out in junior high as the chubby new kid with glasses and freckles, who the popular kids loved to tease or even worse . . . ignore," says the doc. "They should see me now!"

Today, Dr. Vicki maintains a private practice in Melbourne, Florida, and writes articles for a variety of periodicals and Web sites. She has been interviewed or quoted in major publications including *Parenting* magazine, *Reader's Digest*, *First for Women*, and *Woman's World*, networks such as Fox, ABC, NBC, and CBS, and several popular Web sites. Dr. Vicki joined esteemed colleagues Tony Robbins, Dr. Wayne Dyer, and Bill Bartmann as coauthor of *The Power of Team*, the latest in the best-selling series Wake Up and Live the Life You Love. She is an adviser for the Web site parentalwisdom.com and also for MTV/Nickelodeon's parentsconnect.com. She is a clinical consultant for Red Line Editorial, Inc. Not to mention, she's the proud mother of Alex, her 21-year-old son who is pursuing his PhD to become a medical researcher.

With all that she has going for her now, it might be hard to imagine that Dr. Vicki was ever an awkward teen struggling to find her way. But consider this—she's living proof that no matter how bleak things might look now, they do get better. The following stories and Dr. Vicki's guidance will help you discover your own path to happiness and success, becoming the Strong, Beautiful Girl you are meant to be.

Take It from Me

There are a lot of cool things about growing up—you get to go more places, do more things, and be more independent. But one not-so-cool thing is that your new freedom can cause friction at home. Your parents might not share your excitement about having a later curfew or getting attention from boys. They may impose extra rules just when you feel ready for the old ones to loosen up. Still, some girls have the opposite problem. With all the new things happening to their bodies, at school, and with their friends, they may crave the comfort of home and family but be unable to find it.

Adolescence can also be a time when girls start to see their families through a new pair of eyes. Whereas before, a girl might not have considered the differences between her family and other families, in adolescence she might become bothered that her family is too boring, too strict, too weird, or too untraditional. Relationships with parents can change as girls start to see themselves as less of a child, but not yet an independent adult.

Of course, being an only child, being the one in the family who gets picked on, or not getting along with your brothers or sisters can make home life that much more frustrating. Sometimes when I look back on my middle school years, I can't believe how miserable I felt when I was forced to spend time with my family. I thought my mom's voice was annoying, my dad was too uptight, my brother was a moron, and my sisters were wannabes. I dreamt about the day when I would move into my own apartment with no curfew, no chores, and no brothers or sisters going through my stuff. But now that I'm grown up and I live in a different city with all the freedom from my family that I could have dreamed of back then, I miss them a ton. I seriously call my mom every day—just to talk!

It's normal to feel frustrated by your family as an adolescent. It helps prepare you for the independence and responsibility that comes with adulthood. But there are ways to handle your frustrations so they don't cause major problems in your relationships with your family members. I hope the girls in this book will help you think about ways to become your own, more grown-up person without having to fight with your mom or dad about it. Besides, with all the other stuff going on in your life right now, you might want a parent or an older sibling to talk to every once in a while.

XOXO,
Ashley

1

Tight Leash

All families are different. Some are lenient and others are rigid. Some parents let their kids eat dinner in front of the television and others have a 9:00 p.m. lights-out policy even on the weekends. There are upsides and downsides to different parenting styles, but having ultra-strict parents during the middle school years can be especially tough. During a time when she wants independence more than ever, a girl whose parents are very strict is likely to feel stifled. It can be hard to understand the reasons for the rules, and the restrictions may seem unfair. A girl may long for more privacy or control over her own decision-making. She might feel like the only girl not allowed to attend the school dance or the football game. She might resent her mom or dad at times, or find herself lying in order to do things with her friends that are against their rules.

So how does a girl with strict parents get by without pulling her hair out—or someone else's? The fact is, if parents feel strongly about the rules they've set up, the chance of getting them to change their minds is slim. But if she acts responsibly, a young girl can perhaps earn more privileges by earning her parent's trust. Read on to find out what Mila did to reason with her super-strict parents.

Mila's Story

Mila was used to her parents being more involved in her life than most of her friends' parents were. They always attended her school events and made sure she participated in all of the youth activities offered at her church. It really meant a lot to Mila that her parents cared about what she was involved in, but sometimes she felt a little weird about it, too.

> **A young girl can perhaps earn more privileges by earning her parent's trust.**

She was also used to having way more rules than other girls her age. She wasn't allowed to wear the halter tops that had become popular with her girlfriends or watch PG-13 movies, even though most of the kids in her class were already allowed to see the R-rated ones. When she did go over to a friend's house, Mila had a strict curfew, and there were consequences if she came home late.

For the most part, Mila was used to her parents' restrictions and usually didn't react much when they blocked something on the computer or imposed a new rule. Lately, though, she found herself clamming up at the dinner table when they made disapproving comments about her friends' clothing or asked questions about the dating habits of the other kids in her class. It annoyed her that they cared so much about what other people were doing.

Talk About It

- Why do you think Mila's parents want to know what is going on with her classmates?

- How would you feel if your parents asked questions about your friends' personal business?

- Is it fair that Mila has stricter rules than other kids?

Because her mom and dad were so rigid about her not watching certain things, playing violent computer games, or going anywhere without supervision, Mila didn't choose to have friends over very often. When her girlfriends came over to hang out in Mila's room, her mom was always peeking in to see what they were up to. In some ways, it was embarrassing. But Mila

really just wanted the chance to have a little freedom and independence with her friends, so it was easier to stay at Taylor's or Lucy's house.

At her friends' houses, their moms would call Mila's mother to reassure her that everything was fine and that she was being supervised. But then they would disappear and leave the girls to do whatever they wanted. It's not that Mila and her friends were always doing things they shouldn't, but Mila knew that what she was doing was dishonest and she felt guilty about tricking her parents. She knew it would hurt them if they knew she wasn't telling the whole truth, but she also liked the secret life she led when she was away from home. She had a chance to get the independence she wanted. Plus, she figured it must not be too bad if the other moms went along with it.

One night when Mila was at Taylor's, Taylor got her mother to call Mila's mom and say they'd be home baking cookies and playing with Taylor's little sister. When Taylor's mom got off the phone, she laughed a little at how Mila's parents worried so much. Mila laughed too and rolled her eyes, but inside she felt the familiar twinge of guilt.

Talk About It

- Have you ever been around parents who didn't follow the rules? How did it make you feel?

- Have you ever felt like you had a secret life that your family didn't know about? What does that feel like?

- What is making Mila feel the twinge of guilt?

That evening, Taylor had plans for a few boys from school to come over to watch movies. Mila knew they'd be alone in the dark with the boys while Taylor's parents went out. She was excited but nervous about the whole thing. What would she do if one of the boys tried to kiss her? In the back of her mind, Mila couldn't help but think about how angry her parents would be if they knew what she was up to.

But Mila really started to get freaked out when the boys showed up with beer. She became worried that things would get out of control. She tried to pull Taylor aside to talk about it, but Taylor just rolled her eyes and told her not to worry so much.

Talk About It

- **What would you do if you were in Mila's position?**

- **Can you recall a time when you felt uncomfortable because other kids were doing something you knew was against the rules?**

At that moment, Mila wished she could call her parents to come pick her up. She knew they would come right away if she needed them, and that made the twinge of guilt even stronger. But she also didn't want to leave Taylor alone with the boys. She decided to stay until they left. She didn't have any beer and made it clear that she wasn't interested in messing around.

After that evening, Mila understood her parents and their rules a little more than she did before. After all, they probably just wanted to protect her from a dangerous situation. But she still longed for more freedom, and she wished they knew that she could handle herself in a tricky situation such as the one at Taylor's. Even though she was scared that they'd be mad, she decided to tell her parents about what happened. She wanted them to know that she was responsible enough not to do something illegal.

At first, Mila's parents were upset that she had lied to them about the supervision, but in the end they appreciated her honesty and agreed that she had acted in a responsible and safe manner. They didn't want her going over to Taylor's house anymore, but they did agree to let her stay up later when she was having a sleepover, and they said she could even watch some PG-13 movies, as long as they'd reviewed them first.

Mila's parents were upset that she had lied to them about the supervision, but in the end they appreciated her honesty.

Talk About It

- Would you be able to call your parents if you were in an uncomfortable situation, or would you be too scared of getting in trouble?

- Do you think Mila handled the situation in the right way? How would you have done things the same or differently?

Part of the struggle between adolescents and their parents during middle school is really a struggle between the adolescent and herself. A girl with overprotective parents can feel resentful toward them because in her eyes, they aren't allowing her to prove she can be self-sufficient. But no matter how controlling parents are, their daughter will eventually find herself in a situation in which she has to choose between right or wrong, or make a decision for her own or another's safety. Getting those opportunities can help a girl put the overprotective parenting in perspective. If she makes the right choices and successfully takes care of herself, this can give her the confidence she may be looking for from her parents.

In the best-case scenario, she may become more ready to stand up for herself to her parents in a way that will actually get their respect. A lot of girls whose parents won't give them the freedom they are seeking will get angry, throw temper tantrums, or sneak around behind their parents' backs. But in order to loosen the rules and give their daughters more freedom, parents usually need to be reassured that their daughters can handle themselves in a mature and responsible way. Daughters can show that by holding calm discussions with their parents instead of yelling or lying.

Get Healthy

1. If your parents are way strict, don't bother fighting with them. Instead, try to get them to compromise with you.

2. Let your parents know when you faced a difficult situation and made a good decision. If you let your parents know how you are dealing with situations on a day-to-day basis, they will most likely trust you to handle yourself in other situations as well.

3. Make a pact with your parents that you can always call them to pick you up—no matter where you are, what time it is, or what you are doing—no questions asked. The issue is safety first—you should always have a plan to get yourself out of an uncomfortable situation if one arises.

The Last Word from Ashley

While it can be very annoying to have to convince your parents to let you do something that all the other kids take for granted, it can also be reassuring to have parents who are so concerned with your well-being and safety. They've been there, and talking with them openly is a great way to get the issues out on the table. If your parents are the Tight Leash types, try to keep this in mind as you figure out smart ways to earn their trust so you can get them to bend their rules every once in a while.

2

Party Animals

While the girl with strict parents has to work hard to gain her independence, the girl with lenient parents has her own set of issues. Instead of worrying that her friends might think her parents are lame for setting a curfew, the girl with super laid-back parents is likely to have friends over all the time, even when they're not invited. There are few rules and even fewer consequences. At her house, she can stay up as late as she wants, go out with people her parents don't know, and sometimes even drink alcohol or use drugs without punishment. Having fun is the name of the game at the Party Animal house.

But sometimes parents who are so laid back about rules can be too laid back about other things, such as making sure to ask their daughter about the science project she worked so hard on or how she is doing in her classes. And if their daughter is more inclined to spend time alone or with just a friend or two, a house that is always full of people can definitely cause conflict. While it may be fun to be popular and have a cool mom or dad, sometimes a girl wishes her Party Animal parents were more like other kids' moms or dads. Because most of the other kids wish their parents were Party Animals, she might be embarrassed or feel like a dork for admitting that she wants more guidance.

While it may be fun to be popular and have a cool mom or dad, sometimes a girl wishes her Party Animal parents were more like other kids' moms or dads.

Dana's Story

Dana had the coolest parents. Everyone said so. They were really into music and art and totally supportive of whatever Dana wanted to do. Once when she was eight, Dana wanted to paint her room orange and black. Instead of telling her no like most parents would, Dana's parents bought her the paint and handed her a paintbrush so she could live in the Halloween pumpkin bedroom she always dreamed of. They didn't even care when she got paint on the carpet.

There were almost always groups of kids hanging out at the house, whether they were Dana's friends, or her older brother Evan's. She couldn't even remember the last night she had spent with just her parents and her brother! Kids liked to come over to play video games, watch television, or just hang out. Dana's family also had a pool in their backyard, and during the summer months when school was out, it was almost always full of kids, some she didn't even know. Sometimes Dana's mom or dad would hang out with the kids, making jokes about characters on television or telling stories about when they were younger. When they did that Dana noticed that the other kids would hang on every word and laugh at every joke as if her parents were the most fascinating people in the world. Sometimes she felt proud, as if their being cool somehow made her cool too. Other times, she resented them, as if they'd taken over her friends.

Talk About It

- How would you feel if other kids liked hanging out with your parents? Why do you think Dana feels two different ways about it?

- Is it wrong for parents to hang out with their kids' friends? Are there different situations that you think might be okay or not okay?

At Dana's house, the weekends were even crazier than the weeknights. It seemed as if everyone wanted to spend the night. Sometimes Dana didn't even feel like having people over but she felt like she had to. She suspected that sometimes Evan felt the same way, but their parents never seemed to care. They didn't ask Dana much about her schoolwork, the books she was reading, or whether she thought she might like to try dance or tennis lessons. They did, however, ask her if she was making out with any boys or if any of her friends had tried drugs. Dana felt funny when they asked her these questions because her parents seemed almost eager to hear the secrets of her eighth-grade classmates, instead of worried or disapproving.

> **Dana didn't even feel like having people over but she felt like she had to.**

Talk About It

- **How do you think Dana feels about her parents forgetting to ask about her schoolwork? How do you think she feels about their interest in other kids' secrets?**

- **Have you ever felt like you had to hang out with friends or be social when you really just wanted to stay home alone?**

- **Have you ever wished that your parents would take more of an interest in how you were doing?**

One Thursday at school, as Dana sat down in her science classroom, a girl named Rachel came over and sat next to her.

"Hey Dana, do you want to be lab partners?" she asked with a smile. Dana and Rachel weren't really close, but Rachel knew some of Evan's friends and she and Dana talked every now and then.

"Sure, Rachel," Dana replied. She was glad to have a partner.

As Rachel and Dana worked on the assigned lab project, they started talking about their plans for the weekend. Before Dana knew it, Rachel had asked if she wanted to have a sleepover the next night. Dana agreed, and Rachel suggested they have the sleepover at Dana's house.

They ended up having a lot of fun, painting their toenails in Dana's room and talking about the cute boys in their class. They went to sleep kind of early because Rachel said she was tired. That was fine with Dana because she was really sleepy, too.

In the middle of the night Dana woke up suddenly and looked over at Rachel. She wasn't there! She walked down the stairs and around the house looking for her but she couldn't find her. Dana started to get worried that something had happened to her. Finally, Dana opened the door to the garage to see Rachel, Evan, and her parents smoking cigarettes and laughing.

"Hey Dana, honey, come hang out with us," her dad called as Dana turned around to go back into the house. But she didn't feel like hanging out with them. She went back to her room and closed the door, tears stinging her eyes. She felt stupid for crying, but she couldn't help herself. It seemed so clear that Rachel had asked to be her lab partner and suggested a sleepover just so that she could hang out with Evan and her

Talk About It

- How do you think Dana felt about her friend hanging out with her parents and brother?

- What would you do if you were in this situation?

parents. For once, she wished people would like her for herself. And she wanted her parents to try to spend time with her instead of with her friends. Dana felt so distant from her mom and dad that she just didn't know how to ask for what she really wanted.

Talk About It

- Do you think Dana should tell her parents how she feels? What would you say to them if you were in her shoes?

- Are there other ways to handle the situation?

- Do you think it would help if Dana and Evan talked to their parents together?

Sometimes in an attempt to be cooler than the other parents, Party Animals actually push their children away. Dana is desperate for real attention from her parents, not to show them off in front of her classmates. Their behavior has made her feel lonely and unappreciated. It can be really confusing to live in a Party Animal house. On one hand, adolescent girls often crave the excitement of going places they've never gone before or hanging out with boys. On the other hand, they want to be able to look up to their parents and confide in them. In the midst of all the new experiences and emotions that go along with getting older, a girl whose parents are Party Animals might long for a predictable and stable home life.

Besides still secretly wanting her parents to take care of her more, a girl from the Party Animal house might resent her parents for acting young. After all, she's the one who is supposed to be the wild teenager! In an unusual form of rebellion, some girls even end up becoming more like parents themselves. They may be trying to punish their parents by refusing to be their friend or fellow partier. Adolescent girls, in particular, can become very annoyed if their moms try to dress like teenagers, and nasty arguments can erupt.

Get Healthy

1. If you feel like your mom tries to dress your age, explain to her in a nice way why it bothers you instead of getting mad.

2. Don't feel bad about wanting to have your friends to yourself. If your parents are hanging around too much, meet your friends at the movies instead and suggest that you do something with your parents another time—by yourself.

3. Look for other role models, such as coaches and teachers, who can give you grown-up advice when you need it.

The Last Word from Ashley

As much as kids want freedom, they need their parents to be parents. Girls don't want to compete with their moms for attention from boys or worry that their dads are too interested in talking to their girlfriends. But some parents are better than others about defining the boundary between themselves and their kids. Girls can deal with Party Animal parents by talking about what makes them feel comfortable or uncomfortable. In some instances, girls may need to seek other role models from whom they can get good advice. In any case, open communication can help give Party Animal parents a clue about what their kids really want from them.

3

The Foreign Girl

A lot of girls in middle school feel desperate to fit in with their classmates. Having the right shoes, the right cell phone, and knowing the latest expressions can seem all-important in the exclusive world of preteen trends. While most girls have times when they feel like they don't belong, girls who are first- or second-generation immigrants may feel like they are different from their classmates nearly all the time. At home they may speak their language of origin, eat the food of their family's culture, listen to traditional ethnic music, and celebrate the holidays of a religion few at their school have heard of. On top of that, girls from newly immigrated families may have parents with completely different values than girls from families who have been in the United States for several generations. The parents or grandparents might not even speak English.

It is not unusual for a Foreign Girl to feel a culture clash between her home life and her social or school life. For example, her parents might seem extremely conservative compared to other girls' parents, or more influenced by their religion. It can be difficult for a Foreign Girl if her parents have old-fashioned ideas about women's roles that conflict

Girls who are first- or second-generation immigrants may feel like they are different from their classmates nearly all the time.

with American ideas that women and men have equality. She may sometimes resent her parents or feel like she can't identify with her peers. Even though many classrooms have kids from numerous different cultural backgrounds, she may still feel like a minority for not growing up in an "Americanized" family.

Fatima's Story

Fatima was first-generation Moroccan-American. Her parents had married in Morocco and moved to the United States shortly before Fatima was born. Her family spent a lot of time together, especially because everyone had to help out at her family's grocery store.

Fatima liked helping at the store. At school, Fatima was the only one whose family was from Morocco, but at the store she got to meet a lot of kids her age who spoke Arabic. She felt very comfortable with them because they had a lot in common.

Talk About It

- Do you feel more comfortable in some places and with some people than with others? Why is that? What's the difference in how you feel?

- Do you speak a different language at home than at school? What is that like?

Among the Moroccan and Arabic families that Fatima knew, hers was just about average. Her mom worked helping her dad at the shop part-time and took care of the house and kids the rest of the time. Her brothers all wanted to become either doctors or businessmen and her sisters all wanted to get married and have kids.

But at school, Fatima felt like her family was really different. When she got on the school bus with her brothers and sisters in the morning, she felt like the other kids stared at them. Maybe it was the way that they dressed, or maybe it was because they had dark skin but looked different than the other black kids. Sometimes Fatima even thought some of them were afraid that they could be terrorists. And for some reason, it seemed like the other kids treated Fatima and her sisters even more strangely than they did her brothers. During breaks, Fatima could see her brothers playing ball with the other boys, but she would stand with her sisters away from the other girls.

Talk About It

- Why do you think kids stared at Fatima and her family? How do you think Fatima feels?

- Why do you think it's easier for Fatima's brothers to fit in with other boys than it is for Fatima and her sisters to fit in with other girls?

Fatima's social studies class had been learning about freedom of speech and social justice for a few weeks. She liked learning about how much things could change in so little time. The only thing she didn't like was when the students were asked to share their experiences with racism with the whole class. Everyone was supposed to take a turn.

The only thing she didn't like was when the students were asked to share their experiences with racism with the whole class.

Jenny went first. "I saw a black man once on the sidewalk," she said. "He was homeless and I felt really bad for him."

The other students all seemed to have similar stories. When Fatima's name was called, her stomach had twisted into a knot. She didn't know what to say, so she just said, "I don't know. I've never noticed anything."

"Nothing?" said her teacher. Fatima just shook her head. Her teacher looked as if she was going to say

something else, but instead she moved on to the next student.

Talk About It

- Why do you think Fatima chose not to share an experience? What made her feel like she had a knot in her stomach?

- Did Fatima choose the easy way out by avoiding the question? Have you ever done that?

- Have you ever had to deal with racism or prejudice because of your race, culture, or religion? What did that feel like? How did you handle it?

After Fatima left class, she felt weird that she hadn't said anything when it was her turn. For once, she'd been able to avoid having the rest of the kids judge her. At the same time, she kind of felt like she'd lied. She knew her parents had experienced a lot of racism when they first came to the United States. Almost everyone in her Arabic community had some story about being called a "terrorist" by a stranger going by, just because of the way he or she looked.

But Fatima was sick of people treating her differently and drawing attention to herself. She wanted to be included in the gossip on the playground and invited shopping with the other girls. She wanted to fit in with her classmates and not stand out so much. Yet, she still felt guilty.

Talk About It

- Have you ever lied about something because you were afraid of what people would think of you?

- Why does Fatima feel guilty?

- What advice would you give Fatima?

Fatima is in an awkward position. On one hand, she feels close to her family and connected to her culture. On the other hand, her culture makes her feel like an outsider at school. In a way, she is stuck between two worlds. A girl who finds herself in this position will often have difficulty during adolescence, when she is searching to find her own identity. She may have a desire to push her parents and family life away a little bit in order to become more of an individual, and yet she may not fully relate to her peers. In some cases, girls choose to reject their families because they want to fit in so badly. If a girl's culture values family above all else, this can be very painful for the girl, her parents, and even other members of her cultural community. It is important that girls find ways to balance both their cultural values and their unique sense of self.

Get Healthy

1. Get involved in a group for kids your age who share your cultural values. They may be going through similar difficulties at school, so it will give you a chance to talk about it with kids who understand.

2. Ask your parents what it was like to grow up in a different culture. You will probably find

that their experiences were similar in some ways. That might make you feel less alone.

3. Practice being a bit more open with your classmates about your culture instead of feeling ashamed. Bring a traditional treat to your class holiday party. You may be surprised that many of your classmates are more curious than judgmental about where you come from.

The Last Word from Ashley

There are many reasons why girls feel awkward or like outsiders during middle school, but feeling ashamed of your family's cultural background can be really painful. Even though it seems easier to pretend you're just like the other kids and come from the same experiences doesn't mean that's really who you are. In many ways, to reject your family is like rejecting yourself. Fortunately, the fact that schools are becoming more culturally diverse will help make foreign girls feel less weird and more typical. Plus, people who are highly connected to their culture have more community support and a larger social network than many Americans who do not feel ethnically connected. That support and social network can help a Foreign Girl meet friends, find dates when she is older, or even help her find a cool summer job.

4

The Little Mother

It is not uncommon to hear an adolescent girl say, "I wish my parents would just leave me alone!" But what is it like for girls who really are left alone? There are plenty of parents who have to work long or odd hours, so they aren't home at the same time as their kids. Girls who are raised by single parents who work see their mom or dad even less often. That leaves those same girls to take care of themselves, and sometimes their younger brothers and sisters. Girls who have to take care of themselves at an early age quickly learn how to do a lot of adult things, such as cooking, cleaning, or helping younger siblings with homework. Little Mothers may feel proud of all the responsibility they have at such a young age, but they are also likely to feel burdened. Instead of just being a kid, in some ways they have to be their own parent. Plus, running a household leaves less time for schoolwork, friends, and extracurricular activities.

Tanika's Story

Tanika was the oldest kid in her family. She had been taking care of her two little sisters almost every day since she was ten. Tanika's dad didn't live at home and her mom worked nights, so she was responsible for getting them up and dressed in the morning, feeding them cereal, and walking them to the bus stop. Then she took a different bus to the middle school.

After school, Tanika stayed at home with her sisters doing homework and watching television while their mother slept. She always fed them dinner, usually either hot dogs or macaroni and cheese. After they went to bed, Tanika usually stayed up and hung out with her mom before she left for work. They would watch reruns of daytime talk shows and laugh. She liked to spend time with her mom just relaxing. It was her favorite part of the day.

Girls who have to take care of themselves at an early age quickly learn how to do a lot of adult things.

At school, Tanika had a few good girlfriends she ate lunch with every day and sat with during breaks. The girls had many of the same classes and usually talked about their favorite teachers or a really cool science project they had seen. But even though they sat together every day, lately Tanika had felt like she didn't have that much in common with them. They had started talking about boys and shopping, and it didn't seem like they ever had any chores at home. When

Talk About It

- **What do you think of Tanika's daily routine? Do you think it is fair that she has to take care of her little sisters?**

Tanika talked about her little sister's problem with her math homework, they looked at her like she'd just said the most boring thing in the world. Even though they were all in seventh grade, it felt like she was an adult and they were still little kids.

Talk About It

- **Do you have friends with very different responsibilities than you? Do you find that it is sometimes hard to relate to them?**

- **Have you ever felt much older or younger than a friend? Why did you feel that way?**

Tanika was so used to taking care of everything for everyone else that she often found herself helping her classmates who had problems learning the material, or staying after class between periods to help her teachers clean up a messy classroom. Even though her teachers often gave her extra credit for helping in the classroom, Tanika rarely got marks above Cs. She really tried to turn in her assignments on time, but she was usually so busy helping her younger sisters with their homework that she didn't always have time to meet her own due dates. And she certainly didn't have time to stay after school for extra help because she had to get home and take care of her siblings.

One day after her history class worked on a big project, Tanika was erasing the board and putting the markers back in bins. Her teacher, Ms. Davies, said, "Thanks very much, Tanika, for your help."

"You're welcome," replied Tanika.

Then Ms. Davies said something that surprised her. "Tanika, you're such a helpful student, but I wanted to talk to you about your grade. You're getting a D right now in the class. Are you having trouble with the material?"

Tanika didn't know what to say. She had no idea she was doing so poorly. And she was surprised Ms. Davies would care. She couldn't remember the last time a teacher had asked her how she was doing with the material.

She felt a wave of panic. What would her sisters do with no one to take care of them?

"I don't know. I guess I didn't think about it," she mumbled.

"I think it would be a good idea if you came in for some help every day after school."

"But I can't! I have to take care of my sisters!" Tanika yelped.

"Well, your mother is going to have to make other arrangements for your sisters for a little while until your grade improves," Ms. Davies replied.

Tanika could tell that Ms. Davies was dead serious. She felt a wave of panic. What would her sisters

Talk About It

- Is it fair that Tanika's grades are rather poor since she is such a good and helpful student in other ways?

- Why do you think Tanika didn't pay much attention to her grades?

do with no one to take care of them? Then she started to get mad. Why would Ms. Davies punish her when she was the only one who helped clean up? It just didn't seem fair.

When Tanika got home that day, her mom had already spoken with Ms. Davies.

"I heard about your grades," Tanika's mom said.

"She wants me to go in after school. It's totally stupid, but maybe you can get me out of it," Tanika suggested.

Talk About It

- Do you think it is fair that Tanika has to stay after school?
- Besides your parents, who are some of the people you can go to when you need help and support?

"No, Tanika, you need to meet with your teacher. I guess you've been doing too much around the house. You should be focusing more on your schoolwork," her mom said. "I'm sorry."

Tanika was surprised to hear her mom say that she was sorry. She had always felt like taking care of her sisters was supposed to be her biggest priority.

At first, Tanika hated having to see Ms. Davies for help with history. She worried about her sisters, who had to go to an after-school program with kids they didn't know. But after a few times, she started to enjoy herself. Ms. Davies always asked her how she was and seemed genuinely interested in hearing about her sister's math problems. She also started to like not having to be the mom right away every day. It was more fun to learn history one-on-one when she could ask whatever questions she had. One day, after Ms. Davies told her that she'd improved her grade to a B-minus, Tanika felt really happy. It had been a long time since she had worked so hard to do something for herself and no one else.

Talk About It

- **What are some reasons Tanika felt so happy? Why had it been so long since she had done something for herself?**

- **How do you think Tanika felt when her mom admitted she was doing too much around the house?**

No matter what age you are, everyone needs nurturing. Tanika was so used to taking care of everyone else that she wasn't getting attention from anyone, including herself. Luckily, she had a good teacher who recognized that she needed some support or her grades would continue to slip. It can be hard to balance school and family life, especially for a girl with a working single parent. She has way more responsibility than most kids her age. Obviously, it is important that she do a good job taking care of her little siblings, but it's also super important that she keeps up her grades. Girls who put all their energy into taking care of other people tend to forget to take care of themselves. Adolescence is a time when it is healthy for girls to be a little selfish and spend some time thinking about who they are and what they want.

Get Healthy

1. If you feel that you are being given too much responsibility at home, talk to your parents about it. Even though they need your help, they may not know how hard it is on you, or how much your schoolwork or social life is suffering.

2. Every day, spend at least 15 minutes daydreaming about your future. In your dream, you can be anyone you want, have

any job, wear any crazy outfit, and go to the most exotic places you can think of.

3. If your mom or dad works all the time and doesn't have much time for you, look for another adult who is interested in talking to you about your life. Maybe you have a cool aunt or grandma who shares some of your interests.

4. Take time to be a kid. Even if you've got a lot of responsibility, don't feel like you have to automatically grow up. Practice doing the silliest thing you can think of, as long as it's not dangerous.

The Last Word from Ashley

There are a lot of parents who don't get to spend enough time with their kids. This is especially true for single parents who have to work extra hard to support a family on one salary. Unfortunately, adolescent girls sometimes feel like they are moms at age 11 or 12 because their family situation forces them to take care of things at home. While it is useful to learn homemaking skills, it is also good for girls to have a chance to just be kids instead of growing up so fast. Plus, adolescence is exactly the time when girls should be developing their own interests, not just worrying about what everyone else needs or wants.

5

Mom Has a Boyfriend

People used to have much different ideas about family than they do today. In the past, families were thought of as Mom, Dad, and the kids. Sure, there were other types of families, such as those with only one parent or grandparents or aunts and uncles who took on the role of Mom or Dad, but these were seen as the exception to the rule. Now, there are so many families who don't fit the old mold of Mom, Dad, and the kids, that it isn't really seen as the rule anymore. There are tons of kids whose biological parents separated and now have new boyfriends, girlfriends, husbands, or wives. It can be strange at first when Mom or Dad starts seeing some-one new after separating from the other parent. A girl may not be totally comfortable with the idea of a new person trying to play the role or even replace her real mom or dad. She also might feel like she is losing the parent who has the new boyfriend, girlfriend, husband, or wife. And even more terrible, a girl could get stuck in the middle between her parents if the single parent is hurt by the new relationship that the other parent is having. Still others find ways to relate to their single parents better than they did when their parents were still together.

Bri's Story

Bri's parents were divorced. They'd been divorced for so long that she didn't even remember them when they were together. At 12 years old, Bri had always lived Monday through Wednesday with her mom and Thursday and Friday with her dad. She alternated weekends at each parent's house, too. Bri was close to both her parents, but her mom was like her best friend. When it was her mom's weekend, they got cinnamon tea and pedicures, went shopping and out to eat at Bri's favorite restau-

A girl may not be comfortable with the idea of a new person trying to play the role or even replace her real mom or dad.

rant, then rented movies at home. Bri filled her mom in on all the gossip at school, and her mom complained about the weird ladies who worked in her office. Bri always looked forward to weekends with her mom.

A few months after Bri's thirteenth birthday, her mom started seeing a guy that she met at the gym. At first Bri didn't think much of it because her mom sometimes went out with guys, but she never got really serious about them. Usually Bri and her mom just ended up laughing about the odd things the men that she went out with said or did.

Talk About It

- If you have parents who are dating or have dated recently, how did you feel about it? Did you like or dislike the people they went out with?

- What is your biggest fear about their dating? What is the thing you like best?

It didn't take long before Bri realized that her mom's new boyfriend, Mike, was not like the guys her mom had gone out with before. For starters, her mom talked about him a lot, and they had been on many dates. In fact, they had been seeing each other for more than three months, which was longer than any other guy her mom had gone out with before. But Bri really noticed that something was going on when they were at their favorite restaurant and Bri made a joke about Mike's dorky shoes. Her mom didn't laugh like she usually would about the guys she dated. Instead

she just said, "He's a really nice guy." Bri felt awkward then and didn't know what to say.

Talk About It

- Why does Bri feel awkward when her mom says she thinks Mike is nice?

- Why didn't Bri know what to say? What do you think she was afraid to say?

- Have you been in this situation? Was it easy to talk about how you felt? What did you do?

Mike started coming over a lot in the evenings to have dinner with Bri and her mom. He sometimes brought Bri little gifts. Once he brought her a CD of her favorite band, but Bri told him she didn't want it.

"It's pointless. They're already on my iPod," she said. She felt a little bad when she saw that her remark had hurt Mike's feelings, but she shrugged it off.

Talk About It

- Why do you think Bri rejected Mike's gift?
- What advice could you give Bri?

Pretty soon, Bri's mom was spending a lot of time with Mike. She even switched a Saturday with Bri's dad so she and Mike could go out of town together. Bri spent that weekend hanging out with her dad and talking about Mike. She hadn't meant to be unkind, but before she knew it she was making fun of Mike. When Bri's dad laughed along at her jokes, it made her feel better. She even laughed when he made a comment about her mom's poor decision making. She also felt kind of guilty though, like she was choosing her dad over her mom and talking behind her mom's back.

One time when Mike was over, Bri's mom had to run to the store to get some last-minute things for dinner. Alone with Mike in the kitchen, Bri found that she was nervous and didn't know what to talk about.

Talk About It

- How would you feel if your mom decided to spend time with her boyfriend instead of you?

- Do you think it's right of Bri's father to laugh along while Bri makes fun of Mike?

- Have you ever felt like you had to choose one parent over the other?

But when Mike started asking her questions about school, they found that they shared a love of reading, and had even read some of the same books. Bri was surprised to find that she had something in common with Mike.

Over time, Bri got more used to having Mike around. She even liked him a little bit, though she wouldn't admit that to her dad. Mike let her help him grill steaks on the barbeque. Plus, she noticed that her mom laughed more and complained less about work when Mike was around. By the time Bri's mom decided to marry Mike, Bri liked him a lot and was used to having him in her life. A part of her considered him to be family, but she knew that he could never take her dad's place.

A part of her considered him to be family, but she knew that he could never take her dad's place.

Talk About It

- Why doesn't Bri want to admit to her dad that she likes Mike?

- How do you define family? Are there people who you consider family even though they are not your blood relatives?

- Has one of your parents ever remarried? How did you feel about that? Did he or she feel like a second mom or dad?

Ask Dr. Vicki

Girls often struggle to figure out how they should treat the new person in their parent's life. Sometimes a girl may feel like she's in competition with her parent's new boyfriend or girlfriend, so she doesn't lose any of her father- or mother-daughter time. The way a girl feels about new stepparents can depend a lot on how her parents split up. If there is anger between the parents or if she spends more time with one parent than the other, she may have a harder time adjusting. She may try to feel the same way her parent feels so they won't argue. She may also be feeling abandoned by the parent she sees a lot less. Or, if a girl likes the new person in her mom or dad's life, she might feel guilty or worried about hurting the other parent's feelings. It's important to keep in mind that it is alright to still love both your parents in a situation like this, and that loyalty comes from loving them, not how you feel about any other person who might enter your life.

Get Healthy

1. Don't be afraid to tell your parents how you really feel about their new relationship. They are probably expecting you to be a little freaked out, and talking about it can help you and your mom or dad come up with ways to make it easier.

2. Don't feel as if you have to like your mom's or dad's new boyfriend or girlfriend right away. You can get to know them slowly by trying an activity together, such as playing a board game or going for a walk.

3. Tell your mom or dad that even though you know they have someone else in their life now, you still want to spend time just the two of you. Just because things have changed in your parent's dating life doesn't mean your parent-child relationship should have to turn upside down.

The Last Word from Ashley

Even though having parents who divorce can be difficult and painful, a lot of girls find that they end up becoming close with new stepparents. There are many emotions involved when a new stepparent enters a girl's life, but as with most things, talking about issues can help a lot. While at first a girl may be protective of her mom or dad, eventually she can be happy that her parent has found someone with whom to spend time and care about.

6

The New Family

One of the hardest things about having parents divorce is when one of them gets remarried or involved in a new relationship. In the last chapter, Bri struggled to accept her mom's new boyfriend, who would eventually become her stepfather. Sometimes, though, it's not just a parent's new boyfriend or girlfriend that a girl has to learn to live with but an entire new set of brothers and sisters, either from the new stepparent's former marriage, or a new baby born between her parent and stepparent.

During adolescence, a girl is likely to fight with any brother or sister. A lot of kids use sibling arguments as a way to struggle for more privacy and independence, which may be core concerns at adolescence. But when a girl has to take on an entire new family because of a parent's remarriage, especially if she ends up living with them, that struggle can become even more intense. Her stepsiblings might have different habits or rules than she has. She might feel jealous of the attention her parent is giving to a new baby, or to the kids of a new spouse. Or sometimes she might feel that there is so much going on with the new living arrangement, with new people

She might feel that with the new living arrangement, there isn't enough room for her or her needs.

who have their own needs, that there isn't enough room for her or her needs. How does a girl find her place in a changing family? This is the question Beth had to answer.

Beth's Story

Beth's parents had been divorced for a few years. The divorce had surprised Beth at the time because they hadn't seemed terribly unhappy, just not very close to one another. But now that they'd been apart for some time, she understood why they had split up in the first place. They were both in new relationships with people who seemed to be better matches for their personalities. Her mom's boyfriend, Don, was into motorcycles and took her mom on lots of trips. Her dad's fiancée, Jill, was a serious type and very committed to her job, just like he was.

For the most part, Beth was pleased that her parents seemed more content with their new partners. There was only one problem. Beth couldn't stand her soon-to-be stepsisters, Chelsea and Britney. Jill's daughters were eight and ten years old, and talked constantly. Even though Jill seemed so conservative, she spoiled them with attention, clothes, and toys. They even had their own monthly clothing allowance. Beth was used to her parents taking her shopping just once or twice a year for school clothes and the basic supplies.

Talk About It

- **Do you have a stepbrother or a stepsister? How did you feel when they came into your life?**

- **Were your stepsiblings raised differently than you? If so, how do you feel about your different upbringing?**

When Jill, Chelsea, and Britney moved into the house with Beth and her dad, there weren't enough bedrooms for everyone. That meant that Beth had to move into the smaller room in the basement so that Chelsea and Britney could share her old big bedroom upstairs. Even though she still had her own bedroom, Beth couldn't help but be furious that she had to move all of her things out of her own bedroom for the little brats. She complained constantly to her dad about how the basement smelled funny, but the truth was that it bugged her to be all the way downstairs when everyone else was on the second floor.

Since Beth lived most of the time with her dad, she couldn't get away from Chelsea and Britney very

Talk About It

- Did anyone ever move into your house? How did it change things?

- How would you feel if you had to move out of your bedroom to make room for a new stepbrother or stepsister?

- Why do you think it bugs Beth to be in the basement while everyone else is on the second floor?

often. They hogged the television and watched foreign language DVDs that Jill bought for them when Beth wanted to watch music videos. Then they ran around the house speaking in foreign accents. Beth was so annoyed that she thought about moving her stuff over to her mom's house. But she figured her mom was too busy with Don and traveling, and that for Beth to stay there would be an inconvenience. She called her mom anyway to complain about the situation and hoped her mom might invite her to stay there. Beth felt worse when the invitation didn't come.

Beth finally had enough when her dad came home one day with two brand-new laptops for Chelsea and Britney. Jill was so pleased that she kissed Beth's dad right on the lips when she saw the surprise. The girls were excited too, jumping up and down and squealing. Beth's dad scooped them into his arms for a big group hug while Beth watched glumly from the couch.

Talk About It

- Have you ever been in a situation like Beth, not really having a comfortable place to be? What did you do?

- Have you ever felt as though one or both of your parents really didn't want you?

- What advice would you give Beth?

She felt like she was watching another family from a distance, as if she were invisible. She felt anger boiling inside her.

"New computers? Is there anything these two don't have?" Beth said, darkly. Everyone turned to look at her as if they hadn't noticed she was sitting there.

"Well, honey," her dad said, looking sheepish, "you have a computer. That nice desktop in your bedroom."

"The computer in that cave you call my bedroom is from like 1990! It was a hand-me-down from your office!" Beth protested.

"I thought it was working just fine for you," said Beth's dad.

"That's not the point," Beth retorted. "You just bought those spoiled brats two brand-new laptops!"

"My daughters are not brats," Jill stepped in, "and they needed the laptops for school."

Beth hated Jill for interrupting the conversation she was having with her dad. She hated her dad for not seeing how unfair it was, and for treating Chelsea and Britney like they were his own kids.

"This has nothing to do with you, Jill. I'm just sick of this. I'm sick of being treated like I don't count now that you have a new family," Beth finally said to her father before leaving the room.

Later that evening, Beth's dad knocked on her door, and she told him to come in.

Talk About It

- Have you ever felt as though you weren't a part of your own family? Did you ever feel that somebody else had replaced you?

- What would it feel like to watch your mom or dad give an expensive present to your stepsibling, when you'd received nothing?

- Why does Beth hate Jill for stepping into the conversation? Why is she so angry with her dad? What other emotions might she be feeling?

"I'm sorry about earlier," he said. "I had no idea how much it would bother you when I gave the girls new laptops."

"It's not just the laptops, Dad, it's this whole situation. Ever since you and Mom split up, I feel like you're so into your own lives that you don't care about being my parents anymore. I guess I'm just not used to it yet," Beth confided, realizing that it felt good to finally say what she'd been feeling.

"I'll try to do a better job. This is new for me too. But, you know, you are my one and only daughter and I love you very much. Maybe I've been trying so hard to make Chelsea and Britney feel comfortable here that I forgot to make sure you were okay. I'm sorry," said Beth's dad, reaching over to hug her.

Beth felt so much better hearing what her dad had to say. She realized that perhaps all the changes hadn't been easy on him, Chelsea and Britney, or even Jill. She knew it would take some time before life and the house would feel normal again.

Talk About It

- Why did Beth feel good about saying what she'd been feeling? Do you ever keep feelings inside?

- What do you think Beth's father is going through?

- How do you think it feels for Chelsea and Britney to move into a new house with a new stepfather and stepsister?

Often, girls who are dealing with their parents' divorce have hurt feelings and difficulty adjusting to the changes that it brings. A girl may look for someone to blame for her hurt feelings. While Beth probably was truly irritated with Chelsea and Britney, she was also feeling resentful toward them for certain changes that weren't necessarily their fault. It turned out what was actually bothering her was that her father wasn't paying attention to her and she was worried about him leaving her for another family.

Being in a stepfamily can feel lonely, especially if a girl keeps her emotions bottled up inside instead of sharing them. It is important that girls find a way to make a space for themselves in the new arrangement. But sometimes that might require a caring parent's help. It can be reassuring for a girl who is entering into an awkward stepfamily living situation to realize that even if she feels alone, it is most likely not the intent of her parent to ignore her. The parent is likely also trying to adjust. It turns out that most of the time the parent has no idea how their daughter is feeling—until she speaks up or acts up! And, if your mom or dad doesn't know how you truly feel, it's hard for them to make things better!

Get Healthy

1. If you have to move into a new house following a divorce, find a spot where you feel comfortable. It could be anywhere from your bedroom to a tree in the yard to sit under. The important thing is that you make it your own.

2. If you're struggling with sharing your parent with a new sibling, make a date with your mom or dad to spend some quality time alone together.

3. Look for an activity that you could enjoy with your new stepbrother or stepsister. Maybe you both like video games, for example. Spend a little time doing the activity together so you start to feel more comfortable around each other. Eventually, you may even feel comfortable enough to ask them how they have been dealing with their mom or dad's remarriage.

The Last Word from Ashley

Divorce and relating to a new stepfamily is never easy. But girls can make it less difficult by being open about how they feel and finding ways to become more at home in their new surroundings. It may not seem likely in the beginning of a parent's new relationship, but stepparents and stepsiblings could become very important people in a girl's life over time.

7

The Family Joke

In most families, different people take on different roles. Sometimes a girl's role in her family depends on whether she's the oldest, youngest, or middle child. In other families, a girl's role might not be linked to her position as a sibling but instead to certain behaviors her family has come to expect of her. Whereas some girls become the angel who can do no wrong, others feel like they get blamed for everything. The girl who becomes the Family Joke has a unique role. Though she may feel hurt or insecure at times, she may not know how to relate to her family when she's not in trouble. After all, at times negative attention can feel better than no attention at all. That is how Kelly used to feel.

Kelly's Story

Kelly was a middle child in a family of four kids. She had always been louder and more energetic than her brother and sisters. Sometimes she felt as if she just couldn't sit still. Instead she would run around and try to get one of her sisters to play a game or follow her mom around the house while she was cleaning. More often than not, Kelly's mom and siblings rolled their eyes at her and told her to calm down or leave them alone. It happened so often that it didn't even seem like a big deal.

She had always been louder and more energetic than her brother and sisters.

Talk About It

- Has anyone close to you ever asked you to leave him or her alone? How did you feel?

- Is there anyone in your family who reminds you of Kelly? Why?

At school, Kelly found it even more difficult to sit still in class and concentrate on what the teacher

was saying. Aside from playing sports during gym class or drawing and painting in art, Kelly really didn't like school. Bringing home low grades every semester didn't help. Kelly's mom and siblings seemed to think it was funny that Kelly couldn't get better grades in what they thought were easy classes.

"How did you get a D in health class? It's so easy, it's a joke!" her older brother would say, as her mom and sisters laughed along.

"I don't know. It was just so boring." Kelly would respond. Then everyone laughed more. Kelly was not trying to be funny, but she laughed along with everyone else. Even though she was laughing, it hurt a little that she was being laughed at for her poor grades.

The only person who didn't make Kelly feel like a total idiot was her dad. Sometimes he came to her rescue when her family was ragging on her. He would say something like, "My little Kellers is good at a lot of things, but health class isn't one of them," and give her a secret wink from across the kitchen table. His support made her feel like she wasn't a total failure.

Talk About It

- **Have you ever been the target of your family's jokes? What was that like?**

- **How do you think Kelly feels about her dad?**

- **Has anyone ever stuck up for you when others were making fun of you? How did it make you feel?**

As Kelly got older, her grades did not improve, except in gym and art class. She really enjoyed drawing, and loved that gym class gave her a chance to run around and use up all that extra energy without anyone telling her to leave them alone.

Her siblings were excellent students, and Kelly began to think that she just wasn't cut out to get good grades.

But because her grades in other classes were slipping, and because she felt as if gym and art weren't real classes, Kelly started to get really discouraged. Her siblings were excellent students, and Kelly began to think that she just wasn't cut out to get good grades. After a while, Kelly thought it seemed pointless to try to be a better student and stopped studying hard for exams. One day, after failing a history test, Kelly hung the test on the fridge with a magnet. While she was doing it, she hoped that even though she had failed the test, she could at least make her family laugh.

Talk About It

- Have you ever made fun of yourself so that no one else would do it first?

- Have you ever failed a test? How did you feel?

As predicted, Kelly's brother started in with the jokes the moment he saw it. But Kelly's mother didn't laugh. She just shook her head with a disappointed look on her face.

"Gosh, Kelly, it's as if you try to do badly!" her mother said. It was not the response Kelly was expecting. She felt her insides tense up. She felt angry and ashamed at the same time. Kelly stormed out of the house, slammed the door, and plopped down on the front steps. She felt like an idiot for thinking it would be funny to put the test up on the fridge. It seemed as if she always felt like an idiot lately.

Talk About It

- Why was Kelly's mom disappointed? How do you think Kelly felt to know that her mom didn't think it was funny?

- Why is Kelly both angry and ashamed at the same time?

- Have you ever felt as though you had disappointed your parents? What happened?

While Kelly was sitting outside, her dad came out and sat down next to her.

"I heard what happened in there. How are you doing?" he asked.

"I just feel stupid," Kelly replied, looking down.

"I know it's not easy to get teased," said Kelly's dad. "Sometimes when people tease, they are trying to tell you something without saying it outright. Everyone has seen your drawings and knows how talented you are. You do so well in art and gym, so when they see you not trying in other subjects, they get disappointed because they believe you can do better. I'm here to help you, but you have to put some effort in instead of just giving up. It is great to have special talents. But it's important that you try to do well in all your classes, not just the ones you like."

It surprised Kelly to hear that her family thought she was talented. She had assumed that they didn't notice her drawings because she was struggling with other classes. After Kelly's talk with her dad, she thought that maybe her family did notice the things that she liked and was good at. She decided to show her mom and siblings some of the new drawings she'd been working on recently. She hoped that they might respect her more if she shared her real interests with them instead of always talking about what they thought was important.

Talk About It

- What do you think Kelly's family was really trying to tell her?

- What did Kelly's dad mean about being there to help her? What had she given up on?

- Do you have a special talent? Do your family members think it's valuable?

- Have you ever let your grades go because you didn't like the class? What happened?

The Family Joke tends to get recognized for the bad things she does, not for the good things. Even though Kelly was talented in gym and art, her family chose to focus on her problems in her other classes. The danger for a Family Joke is that she may do things that fit with her family's negative image of her, just for the sake of being recognized. Over time, she may see herself as unworthy and untalented. It is important that she break the cycle of looking to get attention in negative ways and start seeking opportunities to do things that make her feel happy and good about herself. It is equally important that she try hard to succeed in all her classes, not just the ones that she enjoys.

Get Healthy

1. Just because your family doesn't think sports are as important as schoolwork is no reason to stop trying your hardest during basketball practice. Look for other people to share your interest. Eventually your parents might start to see how much you enjoy it and begin to support you.

2. Failing on purpose will only hurt you. If you keep trying to do your best, even at the things you dislike or aren't good at, you will feel better about yourself in the long run. Remember the old saying, "If you think you

are going to fail, you will fail," and do the opposite.

3. If your family is ganging up on you, take your parents aside and explain to them how much it bugs you. They may not realize how the family's words affect you. Their teasing may be a way of them trying to tell you something. Make them say what they really mean.

4. Realize that you are ultimately responsible for your own happiness. So if painting and drawing make you happy, keep doing those things, just as long as you try new things every once in a while too!

The Last Word from Ashley

It may seem like your family undervalues your interests, but that does not mean your interests aren't worthwhile. Girls who don't let other people's opinions of them bring them down have the chance to become free thinking, creative, and independent women. If a girl can learn to trust herself instead of trying to match what everyone else thinks of her, then being a Family Joke can help her speak her mind and form original opinions. Have you ever heard the phrase "think outside the box"? Well, there are a lot of former Family Jokes out there who benefited from learning that very important skill.

8

The Girl Who Has It All

Throughout this book, you've seen ways that family relationships can be difficult, annoying, or frustrating. But what about the girl who seems to get everything she wants from her family? Believe it or not, there are some girls out there who have two adoring parents ready to provide anything their daughter needs. The opposite of the Family Joke, this girl is the Family Angel. In her parents' eyes, she can do no wrong. If she needs a new dress for the school dance, her mom suggests they shop at the most expensive designer boutique to find it. If she fails a test, her dad calls the teacher to complain that the material was too difficult. They support her success and her beauty, sometimes even more than they support themselves.

But even the Girl Who Has It All may find that too much attention can be too much to take. She may want to do her own thing sometimes rather than having to always involve her parents. Plus, classmates aren't nearly as loving and supportive as parents, so the Family Angel may be in for a rude awakening when she discovers that she can't always get what she wants outside the safety of her home.

Cleo's Story

Cleo was the only child of two first-generation Greek parents, and they loved her more than anything. Her parents had worked hard and made good money, and they spent that money on their precious daughter. She not only shopped in the designer section, she was actually fitted for the designers' new collections each season. When Cleo decided she wanted to be a painter, her parents had her room redesigned to look like an artist's studio. When she changed her mind and decided to become a

Even the Girl Who Has It All may find that too much attention can be too much to take.

horseback rider instead, they had no problem buying her a horse and paying for it to be boarded at a local stable. It seemed they would do anything to make her happy.

But there was a problem. Cleo couldn't seem to stay happy for long. Sure, new dresses and shoes were fun for a few days, and the rush she got throwing a huge bash complete with a live band for her fourteenth birthday lasted at least a week or two. But other than passing moments of excitement, she felt bored and anxious. Whenever she felt that way, she and her mom would go shopping for what they liked to call "retail therapy."

Talk About It

- Do you know someone who can have anything she wants anytime?

- Why does Cleo feel bored and anxious? Is "retail therapy" a good way to solve her negative feelings? What could she do instead?

- What would you do if you could have everything you wanted?

Part of the reason why Cleo felt bored and anxious had to do with her social life. She knew almost everyone at school and had a lot of acquaintances, but few of them were really close friends. She had a rotating door of girlfriends who she'd hang out with all the time for a few weeks, but they'd lose touch quickly. It wasn't as if these girls avoided her. They just stopped inviting her to things or calling her to hang out with them. Cleo would then just end up hanging out with her parents.

Cleo had been particularly hurt by her friendship with a girl named Gayle. She and Gayle met in class when Gayle complimented Cleo's new boots. She and Gayle started to go shopping with Cleo's mom's credit card after school a few times a week and had a lot of fun. Cleo started to think of Gayle as her best friend.

One day when Cleo and Gayle were shopping, Cleo's mom came to pick them up an hour early, just as Cleo was about to try on a really cool pair of jeans. She was so annoyed with her mom for picking them up early that she screamed at her in the parking lot, right in front of Gayle.

Cleo suddenly felt like a little kid throwing a temper tantrum, and she felt ashamed.

"You just show up without even calling my cell phone! Didn't you think we might be busy?" Cleo screamed at her mom.

"I drive you around wherever you want to go and you don't seem to even appreciate it!" her mom yelled back, looking hurt.

"I'm supposed to appreciate you picking us up an hour early?" Cleo said sarcastically. She tried to make eye contact with Gayle about how stupid her mom was acting, but Gayle wouldn't look at her. Cleo suddenly felt like a little kid throwing a temper tantrum, and she felt ashamed.

Soon after the fight, Gayle didn't seem as interested in going shopping anymore. When Cleo asked her to go, Gayle said it was boring to go and watch someone else shop for clothes when she couldn't get anything for herself. Gayle started hanging out with other girls instead. Cleo was so upset about the situation that she complained to her parents.

"Well, there will always be girls who are going to be jealous of someone as pretty and smart as you," said her dad.

Talk About It

- Have you ever exploded at your mom or dad the way Cleo did? How did it feel at the time and how did it feel afterward?

- Why do you think Cleo tried to make eye contact with Gayle? Why do you think Gayle wouldn't look at her?

- Do you think that Gayle being bored shopping is the only reason she stopped hanging out with Cleo?

"You don't need Gayle to go shopping when you've got me!" said Cleo's mom.

Cleo knew her parents were trying to make her feel better, but for some reason it just didn't seem to help. She wanted to hang out with people her own age instead of her mom.

Talk About It

- **What do you think about how Cleo's mom and dad reacted to her problem with Gayle?**

- **Have you ever tried to talk about a problem that your parents tried to fix or make less important than it was? Did it help?**

For a while, Cleo continued to shop and spend time with her parents since there was no one else around. Her feelings of boredom and anxiety continued too. Finally she picked up the phone and called Gayle. Gayle answered.

"Hey," said Cleo. "I just wanted to say I'm sorry if you were bored going shopping. Do you want to hang out and do something else?"

"Like what?" Gayle answered, sounding interested.

Cleo decided that for once, the choice would not be hers. "It doesn't matter to me. What do you feel like doing?"

"You can come over and watch television with me and Tina if you want," offered Gayle.

"Okay, that sounds fun." Cleo was smiling. She felt so happy to have her friend back that she made a promise to herself not to screw it up by acting like a little kid this time.

Talk About It

- **Did Cleo do the right thing by calling Gayle and apologizing?**

- **Why did Cleo decide to let Gayle make the decision about what they did?**

A girl who can do no wrong in her parents' eyes is at risk of having problems with friends. She is so used to getting what she wants with no real effort that she will have a hard time understanding when other people don't bend over backward for her. Worse, she may feel less capable of taking care of herself because her parents are always there to take care of her. Over time, she trusts herself less to take care of her needs, or even to know what she really wants, and that causes feelings of anxiety and insecurity.

Girls benefit from peer relationships that give them a chance to see themselves as individuals through the eyes of classmates, from a different perspective than family relationships. A girl will always be the daughter when she is with her parents, but when she is with her friends she gets a chance to spread her wings and discover her individuality.

Get Healthy

1. Everyone needs time to think. If your parents are overbearing, find ways to take some quiet time for yourself, whether that means drawing, reading a book, or taking a walk.

2. Try to balance time with family and time with friends. Your mom may be cooler than any other girl at school, but it is still a good idea to make friends with kids your own age who are going through the same things that you are going through.

3. Go with the flow instead of running the show—you may learn something or discover a new interest. Make sure that in any relationship you have that each of you gets to make some of the decisions and be in charge some of the time.

4. Be more mature than to blow up at someone. If your mom makes you mad, try calmly explaining to her why you are frustrated instead of starting a yelling match. You might find that she listens to you better that way.

The Last Word from Ashley

No girl gets her own way all the time. Unfortunately, it might take the girl who has everything a little bit longer to figure that out than the rest of us. She spends so much time with her parents that she may even struggle trying to relate to girls her own age. Even though it might be a challenge to hang out with her peers, it is the best way for her to get connected with herself and learn to be more independent instead of relying on others to take care of her.

9

The Annoying Sibling

Have you ever tried to imitate a person you admire? There is absolutely nothing wrong with looking up to someone and trying to be like that person. In fact, that is a good thing! However, if you have a younger sibling who copies your every move, it can feel quite different. From hanging around all the time to taking your things without asking, younger brothers and sisters can be a real test of patience. Even if a sibling is just a few years younger than you, it can feel like the biggest difference! But believe it or not, as you and your siblings grow up and mature together, the gap between your ages will seem smaller and smaller.

Brothers and sisters can be some of the best friends you'll ever have—they know you really well, and they still put up with you despite all that! You might have an older brother to look out for you, or an older sister who listens to you and gives you advice. On the other hand, you may be the oldest in the family and find yourself

Getting through the growing up years with siblings can be one of the biggest challenges.

feeling protective of the younger kids. Getting through the growing up years with siblings can be one of the biggest challenges you will go through, but try to look at the positive side—being an older sister is good practice for learning how to be responsible and mature. It gives you chances to learn to care for others, develop patience, and even to be a role model for someone younger than you. That's what Kate came to find out.

Kate's Story

Kate was the oldest of three children. Her mom and dad were the warmest, most caring parents she could ever ask for, and she had a really good relationship with them. But when her baby sister, Carrie, was born, Kate suddenly had to share a bedroom with her younger sister, Abby.

It wasn't so bad at first because Kate and Abby got along really well. Even though Kate was about to start junior high in the fall, Abby was only going into first grade, which meant that Kate got to do all kinds of little kid stuff with her sister. Kate liked to read to

Abby, and she would take her to the park across the street and push her on the swings. But after a while things started to get really tough. Kate couldn't stay up late talking on the phone with her friends anymore because Abby went to bed so early. And sometimes, Kate just wanted to be alone in her room, away from her little sister.

That summer, Kate had finally gotten permission from her parents to start wearing a little makeup. She and her friends would gather in Kate's room, each bringing over some eye shadow, lip gloss, or mascara. Sometimes they even brought clothes over and tried on each other's tops and jeans to make different outfits. They practiced a lot so that they would be able to start junior high looking a little older. The only problem was that since Abby had moved into Kate's room with her, she had really started to bug Kate and her friends by copying everything they did.

Talk About It

- Why did it bother Kate that Abby was copying her and her friends?

- Do you have younger siblings? Do they ever get on your nerves? What do you do about it?

- Did you ever have to share a room? How did you handle it?

One day, Kate's friend Juliet brought over some of the brand-new makeup she had just bought from the expensive department store counter at the mall. Juliet was super excited to try it out. She and Kate put the eye shadow on each other, and then tried on some of the lipstick. They both agreed that they looked gorgeous! Just then, the doorbell rang and they went downstairs to see who it was.

All she wanted to do was yell at Abby, to explode at her and make her feel terrible for what she had done.

When they came back up to Kate's room, they couldn't believe what they saw. Abby was sitting in front of the mirror with lipstick all over her mouth, holding Juliet's brand-new mascara in her hand. Even worse, they saw that Juliet's eye shadow had spilled out of its case and was all over the floor.

"Kate!" screamed Juliet. "Look what your sister did! I can't believe you let her do that! Why can't she just leave us alone?"

Juliet quickly scooped up what was left of her makeup and stomped out the door. Kate was so embarrassed she didn't know what to say.

Talk About It

- Why do you think Abby put the makeup on? Do you have a younger sister who gets into your stuff?

- What do you think about how Juliet reacted?

- Why did Kate feel so embarrassed? Has your brother or sister ever embarrassed you? How did you deal with it?

Kate could feel her face turning bright red. All she wanted to do was yell at Abby, to explode at her and make her feel terrible for what she had done.

"Abby!" she shouted. "What are you doing? I told you to leave us alone!"

Abby started to cry. Just then, Kate's mom came into their room and saw Abby with the makeup all over her face. "What happened here, girls?" asked her mom. "Why are you shouting?"

Kate told her mom everything, and with tears running down her face she threw herself on her bed. She was so angry with her sister for what she did. All she wanted was to get away from Abby, but sharing a room made that really hard to do.

Talk About It

- **What do you think about Kate's reaction to what happened?**

- **Was there a better way that Kate could have handled things?**

- **How would you have reacted if you had been in Kate's shoes?**

The next morning when Kate went downstairs for breakfast, her mom was waiting for her.

"Kate," she said, "I want to talk to you about what happened yesterday. I understand that you were frustrated with Abby for what she did. Your father and I have punished her for getting into your friend's things without asking. But even so, it was not okay for you to yell at your sister."

"I couldn't help it!" protested Kate. "She embarrassed me! I was so angry with her for making me look so stupid."

"I understand that, Kate, but your younger sister looks up to you very, very much. She admires you, and she wants to be like you! Don't you see what an honor it is that your little sister sees you as a role model?"

Kate was surprised. She had never really thought about it that way. It had seemed to her that Abby was wearing her clothes and putting on her makeup just to annoy her. It really was a cool thing that her little sister looked up to her. It made her feel a little more mature. But still, she wished Abby would stay out of her stuff.

Talk About It

- How do you think knowing she is admired will change the way Kate acts toward her sister?

- What are some of the responsibilities that come with being a role model?

- Are you a role model to any of your siblings? How do you feel about that?

- Do you have older siblings whom you look up to? Why?

Brothers and sisters: you can't stand to have them around, and yet you wouldn't want to live without them. It's quite all right for you to tease them, but you would be the first one to defend them if anyone else tried to pick on them. It's not always easy to be the big sister, especially when the younger kids can be so annoying. And, let's face it—it's not like you got to decide if you wanted any siblings; it was just assumed that you would be delighted to have someone else around to share your stuff, like your room and your parents' attention. Now that's annoying! It is perfectly normal and definitely okay to feel these emotions about your siblings. It's even okay to sometimes wish that you were an only child, or that your younger siblings weren't around. Most kids think that way some of the time. But at other times you might be like Kate, discovering that there is a real soft spot in your heart for your younger siblings. And knowing that the little kids are looking up to you and wanting to be like you might help you feel and act a little more grown up.

Get Healthy

1. Yelling rarely helps in any situation. If your first reaction is to explode at someone, take a few moments to calm down before

you say anything. Thinking before you speak can work wonders in any relationship!

2. If you have younger siblings, remember that they are watching you closely. This is a lot of extra responsibility. Like Kate, it is good to realize that younger brothers or sisters are not always out to annoy you when they copy you; they may just be trying to be like you and that is a real compliment!

3. If you do have to share a room with your sister and you want some privacy, talk about it. Ask her if you could have a schedule or a system to make sure that each of you gets some alone time in your own personal space.

The Last Word from Ashley

Siblings can drive you crazy one minute and be your best friend the next. As an adult, it is so good to have close relationships with your brothers or sisters! It is great to have someone who can look back at childhood and adolescent memories with you and laugh along. If you are in a tough stage with a sibling right now, find comfort in knowing that when you are both adults, the little sibling quarrels will matter less, and the strong family bond will matter a lot more.

A Second Look

No matter who your family is, you have to admit that deep down you totally love them, even if there are times when you don't particularly like them. After all, no one is going to tell you exactly what they think like your family will.

The girls in this book came from divorced families, families that looked or acted differently than everyone else, parents who were way too strict, and those who were too lenient. Even though everyone's family was so different, the girls shared one thing in common. They were all looking for a way to grow and become more independent, while still taking cues from the family that had raised them.

Even the strongest and closest families tend to struggle during a daughter's adolescence. Parents want to protect their little girl but can't deny that she is quickly becoming a young woman. A daughter is excited about getting older and breaking free of the limits of little girlhood but still wants to know her family is there if she needs them. On the flip side, some families push a girl to grow up too soon, before she's truly ready to face the world as an adult.

Whatever your family issues—and trust me, we all have them—I hope this book made you think about smart ways to give your family a clue about what you're going through, and helped you learn to understand where they're coming from a little better too. They're not perfect, but they're your family!

XOXO,
Ashley

Pay It Forward

Remember, a healthful life is about balance. Now that you know how to walk that path, pay it forward to a friend or even to yourself! Remember the Get Healthy tips throughout this book, and then take these steps to get healthy and get going.

- Prove to your parents that you deserve their trust. Respect their rules and show them through smart, mature decisions that you can handle more responsibilities, and more privileges!

- Look for ways that you can spend time with family and friends together, to let your parents get to know your friends. But on the flip side, it is important to have time alone with friends, without your parents, to just have fun and be a kid.

- Join a diversity group to meet people your age who come from different backgrounds. Be aware of cultures around you other than your own. Take an active interest in others.

- Communicate with your parents if you feel that they are working too much and don't have enough time for you. They may not even know you feel this way. Let them know that spending time with them is important to you!

- If you find yourself in a situation that makes you uncomfortable or you feel unsafe, don't be afraid to call your parents and ask them to come get you. Make a secret code that you could say on the phone to let your parents know you need to be picked up without alerting your friends to your decision. "How's Uncle Bob?" could be the signal that you need a ride.

- If you are put into a new family situation through divorce or remarriage, try your best to keep an open mind. Chances are, everyone else in the situation is having a hard time adjusting to the changes, too. Take time to talk through these changes with your mom or dad, and make sure to let them know how you are feeling.

- Everyone needs time to think. Take time alone doing something you enjoy, whether that means going for a bike ride or just lying on your bed dreaming about the future.

- Get in the habit of thinking before you speak. In an emotional situation, or if you feel a fight with a family member brewing, try calmly explaining your emotions instead of yelling at someone. The people you are talking to will be less likely to yell if you speak kindly and listen to their side, too.

Additional Resources

Selected Bibliography

Bode, Janet. *For Better, For Worse: A Guide to Surviving Divorce for Preteens and Their Families.* New York: Simon & Schuster Children's Publishing, 2001.

Kelly, Marguerite. *Marguerite Kelly's Family Almanac: The Perfect Companion for Today's Family—a Helpful Guide to Navigating Through the Everyday Issues of Modern Life.* New York: Fireside, 1994.

Rosenberg, Ellen. *Get a Clue!: A Parents' Guide to Understanding and Communicating with Your Preteen.* New York: Henry Holt and Company, LLC, 1999.

Further Reading

American Girl. *A Smart Girl's Guide to Sticky Situations: How to Tackle Tricky, Icky Problems and Tough Times.* Middleton, WI: American Girl, 2002.

Holyoke, Nancy. *The Big Book of Help.* Middleton, WI: American Girl, 2004.

Mosatche, Harriet S., and Elizabeth K. Lawner. *Girls: What's So Bad About Being Good?: How to Have Fun, Survive the Preteen Years, and Remain True to Yourself.* New York: Three Rivers Press, 2001.

Rutledge, Jill Zimmerman. *Dealing with Stuff That Makes Life Tough: The 10 Things That Stress Teen Girls Out and How to Cope with Them.* New York: McGraw-Hill, 2003.

Web Sites

To learn more about healthy family relationships, visit ABDO Publishing Company on the World Wide Web at **www.abdopublishing.com**. Web sites about family are featured on our Book Links page. These links are routinely monitored and updated to provide the most current information available.

For More Information

For more information on this subject, contact or visit the following organizations.

New Moon

New Moon Girl Media
2 West First Street, #101, Duluth, MN 55802
800-381-4743 or 218-728-5507
http://newmoongirlmedia.com
An advertisement-free publication for girls, this group seeks to encourage girls to speak up and be heard.

Pearls for Teen Girls

2100 North Palmer Street, Milwaukee, WI 53212
414-265-7555
http://www.pearlsforteengirls.com
Pearls for Teen Girls is a community program focusing on self- and skill-development to increase confidence and better life choices.

Glossary

confide

    To talk about private matters with someone you trust.

culture

    The ideas, traditions, and behaviors belonging to a certain group of people.

curfew

    A designated time to be home.

foreign

    From another country.

immigrant

    A person who moves permanently to one country from a different country.

judge

    To form an opinion or an idea about someone or something.

lenient

    Tolerant, not strict.

nurture

    To develop, support, and encourage. To tend to the needs of another.

overprotective
Strict or overbearing.

racism
The belief that one race is superior to another.

resent
To feel angry, hurt, or annoyed about something.

role model
A person you look up to or admire.

strict
Imposing many rules.

Index

About the Author

Ashley Harris lives and works in Chicago, Illinois, where she completed an MA from the University of Chicago. Her research focused on how Web culture has impacted adolescent girls' body image and sense of identity. Her work has appeared in *VenusZine* and *Time Out Chicago*. She enjoys live music, bike riding, and spending time with the many friends whose experiences helped her write this book.

Photo Credits

Paul Kline/iStockphoto, 13; Stephen Derr/Getty Images, 17; LWA/Dann Tardif/Getty Images, 24; iStockphoto, 27, 74; Kraig Scarbinsky/Getty Images, 32; Image Source/AP Images, 35, 57, 89, 94, 96; Felix Alim/iStockphoto, 37; Yellow Dog Productions/Getty Images, 42, 94; Jaren Wicklund/iStockphoto, 45; Andres Peiro Palmer/iStockphoto, 52; Jupiterimages/AP Images, 54; James Pauls/iStockphoto, 62; Hummer/Getty Images, 65; Dylan Ellis/Getty Images, 66; Cat London/iStockphoto, 78; Rich Legg/iStockphoto, 84